FRENCH CHATEAU STYLE

*Inside France's Most Exquisite
Private Homes*

Catherine Scotto
Photographs by Marie Pierre Morel

PRESTEL
Munich · London · New York

Foreword by Jean-Louis Remilleux

The book you have just opened is unlike any other. This is no informal listing of more or less famous buildings, chosen with the aim of reuniting world-famous châteaux peopled by the ghosts of statuesque monarchs. Nor is it an illustrated directory of high society featuring an endless succession of illustrious aristocrats. This is because the châteaux that have been selected are owned by true aficionados, who have given themselves body and soul to their restoration in terms of time, energy, and money. Moreover, the authors, Catherine Scotto and Marie Pierre Morel, have deliberately chosen châteaux in accordance with their own tastes, resulting in a passionate and subjective look at properties too long ignored, all in keeping with their idea of living art the French way, a coming to terms with beauty, history, and poetry. With a smidgen of fantasy thrown in for good measure.

I often say to the numerous visitors on the occasion of Heritage Days, generous in their praise and congratulations when confronted with a recently restored château: the inheritors themselves have no merit as such! I can imagine the anguish and subsequent calvary of those who discover, on the reading of a will, that they are the owners of a ghost ship from times past, sailing through the overgrown lawns of an abandoned demesne. Often, they have neither the means nor the will to embark on a life of sacrifice, and they are obliged, against their will and that of their entourage, to maintain the inheritance and to make sacrifices for it, all for the sake of family honor. It's a different matter entirely when it comes to those who have *chosen* the life of château owner, who have done everything to make a dream come true, who awake each morning under a ceiling several meters high, and who look through their windows and see the reassuring symmetry of a French garden, or the foibles of an English one. Although it goes without saying that such days are often preceded by sleepless nights during the restoration itself: when there seems to be no light at the end of the tunnel, when the subsidies don't arrive on time, when a ceiling collapses, when a leak reveals a roof in need of repair, when the cold seeps under the windows, or when the fireplace in the *grand salon* threatens to burn everything down … but surely this is a small price to pay for the freedom to take up a challenge deemed impossible, to live a different type of life in pursuance of an ideal of beauty, space, and harmony?

Our contemporaries' passion for châteaux and for heritage in general continues to grow, an enthusiasm that has had remarkable results throughout France. Whether it be a taste for history on a large or small scale (this in a world that has lost its bearings), or a taste for nature, trees, gardens, or birds (on a planet urbanized to the nth degree), or, again, a taste for furniture, paintings, eighteenth-century bibelots, or interior decoration of all epochs: all of these things conspire to make the public zealous to discover these gardens of Eden, denuded as they are of nostalgia. It is the same sort of zeal, coupled with supplementary courage and determination, that drives the owners to tie their destiny to that of a monument.

The owners, in dedicating themselves to a new lease of life for the châteaux that you are about to discover, have dedicated themselves not to a dusty memory, but to an ideal. They have gambled on the future, namely the transmission and the sharing of architecture of originality, as well as an exceptional *savoir-faire*, an emblematic work of art, an unknown epoch—in short, the rescuing of a small haven of beauty, which in time may become a reference point for future artists. In doing so they have also rescued the natural environment surrounding the châteaux. Lastly, they have often given new hope to a community, a village, or a region. One thinks of the countless enterprises, talents, young people, and the unemployed who have found an unexpected and worthwhile activity on heritage construction sites. Not to mention the many local businesses that have reopened as the village château begins to attract thousands of visitors.

If today's châteaux owners are lucky enough to live the romantic dream to which this magnificent book renders homage, they are at the same time champions of a priceless optimism, of the sort usually associated with wise fools and children.

Jean-Louis Remilleux is a journalist, filmmaker, château owner and collector. He lives in the Château de Digoine in Burgundy (see p. 216).

Château de Marcellus
Valley of the Garonne

It took just a few months for Catherine and Samuel Roger to rescue the treasure-trove that is Marcellus from oblivion. Situated on the banks of the Garonne, life in the château flows by at a gentle pace, surrounded as it is by antiques and a refined, preserved past.

Larger than Life

A passionate antique dealer, Samuel Roger admits that he would never have embarked on such an adventure without the support of his wife Catherine. For several months, the couple had been looking for a location big enough to install their vast collection of statuary. The idea of leaving the Paris region in order to live in the South-West had been under consideration for a whole summer; discovering Marcellus decided them. As I stroll with Samuel Roger (a specialist in architectural antiques and garden ornaments) through the maze of the historical monument that he acquired in November 2020, he admits to being no longer daunted by life in a château, even confessing to having become completely addicted to his new, unorthodox way of life.

At long last, the proud owner of a château! This family of antique dealers would seem to have been destined to live in marble halls—and yet, nothing had quite turned out as expected. Michel Roger, Samuel's father, had begun selling antiques when he founded *Pierres d'Antan* (Stones of Yesteryear) in Houdan in the 1980s. He was successful to the point of opening his own auction room in order to sell his acquisitions. A devotee of heritage, he died at the age of seventy without having realized his dream of living in a château. The somewhat stormy relationship between father and son had prompted Samuel Roger to branch out on his own. In 1992 he founded *Origines*—his own company, which designs interiors and deals in antiques—and twelve years later opened a gallery in the prestigious *Carré Rive Gauche* in the rue des Saints-Pères in Paris. However, meeting Catherine prompted him to change tack. Marcellus had been on the market for six years: they had found that elusive pearl of great price.

The north façade of this elegant structure, built in 1773, juts out over the *Canal du Midi* and, on the south, has a view of the small village of Marcellus. The thirty-four-hectare property has several outbuildings, which the new owners immediately set about renovating. Samuel Roger has placed a part of his collection of fireplaces, fountains, parapets, and other antiques in the tenanted farm. Monumental sculpture and urns are dotted around the park, awaiting new owners. The farmhouse and shed for storing casks will be transformed into reception areas with guest rooms and a spa, while a line of natural cosmetics will be made on site. Catherine Roger is supervising the decoration, in particular the eighteenth-century château's numerous rooms, which are to be equipped with new bathrooms. The reception rooms on the ground floor are so beautiful that they will hardly be restored at all, with a view to safeguarding the subtle nuances of the original paneling. The elaborate decor of the main living room, modified in the nineteenth century, is in a constant state of metamorphosis. Statues and furniture exist in a state of perpetual flux in the antique dealer's perfectly choreographed ballet of sales and acquisitions.

The couple have found a setting on the banks of the Garonne that lives up to their expectations, which is to say the creation each day of moments of ephemeral magic, with a view to reviving Marcellus's splendor.

The story of Marcellus

The Château de Marcellus, situated in a strategic and imposing location in the Valley of the Garonne, belonged to the d'Albret family from the fourteenth century on. At the end of the sixteenth century one of its famous descendants, King Henry IV of France and Navarre, sold it to one Aymeric de Gasq. Only the foundations had survived when a *château de plaisance* was constructed in 1773 for the new owners, André Joseph de Martin du Tyrac de Marcellus, and his wife Suzanne Angélique de Piis-Beauséjour, following the plans of the Bordeaux architect Richard François Bonfin. The Count of Marcellus, a knight of the Order of Malta, was wealthy, the decor of his château splendid. A life of luxury was the norm in Marcellus, where an army of servants was employed.

In 1820, at the time of the Restoration, the Count's grandson, Count Lodoïs de Marcellus, Secretary to the Embassy at Constantinople, traveled to Milos and negotiated the purchase of the famous *Venus de Milo* for Louis XVIII the following year. Some time later Charles X gave Lodoïs a copy as a token of gratitude. This plaster statue, based on the original found in the Louvre, was to be seen in the Great Salon until 2020, when the château was sold by the Chérade de Montbron family (direct heirs of the Marcellus family) to the antique dealer Samuel Roger. The celebrated *Venus* is currently in storage, awaiting a new owner.

Thanks to having had just three different owners in six centuries, the demesne has emerged relatively unscathed. The *Base Mérimée*, a database of the architectural and monumental heritage of France, provides an accurate description of the contemporary restoration of the statuary, the provision of new marble paving in the vestibule, and the addition of columns and double arches in the Great Salon in 1813, as well as the crowning of the façade with three pediments in 1860. A fire, which destroyed a portion of the roof space in 1954, was followed by a reconstruction of the roof according to the original specifications.

Samuel Roger and his wife never tire of exploring the slightest hidden nooks and crannies of their new acquisition and continue to make agreeable discoveries. A well, dug thirty-eight meters into the bedrock, continues to supply water to the entire household. The original and perfectly preserved kitchens close by, where the Rogers organize candlelit dinners, are equipped with a bread oven and an enormous fireplace, complete with its own turning spit in perfect condition. In the attic, Catherine has discovered the original beds, their printed fabric bedspreads barely faded, which she is gradually restoring for use in the bedrooms. A little further off a greenhouse, currently choked by brambles, will shortly house a collection of orchids.

The tenanted farm, a barn-like structure in the *landais* style dating from 1752, is now home to the workshop where Samuel carries out restorations. All hands are on deck for the renovation of the tobacco-drying shed, which is to be transformed into an art gallery by the winter of 2021. The story of Marcellus, like a fairy tale, continues apace.

11
In 1772 the two north-facing pavilions supported by arcades were linked together by a terrace overlooking the Canal du Midi, boasting a wide panorama of the Valley of the Garonne.

12
Two allegorical terracotta figures by Du Maige dating from the end of the eighteenth century, placed on Languedoc red marble plinths, frame the door of the salon. The vestibule in Marcellus, to which a French window was added in the nineteenth century, was repaved with marble at the same time.

13
Detail of the entrance gate to the château.

15

14–15

Graced with arches and pillars in the nineteenth century, the Great Salon opens out onto the terrace. The aim is to preserve the subtle grayish hues of its paneling. Note the riding-school horse modeled on one dating from Louis XIV's reign, carved in Louis XVI style during the reign of Napoleon III, which is placed at the entrance to the salon; carved from a single piece of wood, it stands on a plinth dating from the Empire. To the left can be seen a bust of Molière in polished plaster, dating from the nineteenth century. A bronze nineteenth-century faun has been placed on the floor. To the right we can see a sixteenth-century *cathedra*, or bishop's chair, in painted wood and gilt.

16

A niche that formerly housed the famous replica of the *Venus de Milo* is now home to a little window seat in Louis XVI style, dating from the reign of Napoleon III. To its right, a marble *Harvest Girl* by Alfred Boucher, dating from the late nineteenth century. Then, from left to right: *Young Girl Bathing* by Frédéric Brou, dated 1905; a monumental plaster bust of *Marianne* (1876), and a nineteenth-century architect's easel made by Maison Vivenox, Brussels.

17

A leather rhinoceros, made in England in 1960, stands guard in front of the smaller salon.

18
One of the first-floor rooms, in the process of being restored.

19
Now posing majestically in one of the suites, this four-poster bed from the Bordeaux region, complete with original drapes, was discovered by Catherine Roger in the attic. It is framed by two Chinese candelabras on guard duty, awaiting restoration.

19

20

22

20

The bread oven in the main kitchen is still in working order, as is the large fireplace. It is at its most agreeable at sunset, and the new owners quickly set up shop there, since it's easy to heat, and regularly host charming candlelit dinners.

21

The former stone oven used for preparing vegetables is to be restored and whitewashed before being pressed into service as soon as the future terrace connecting the kitchen to the swimming pool is ready. In this way this strategic site will once again assume its central role, as it did during the golden age of Marcellus.

22

Since 1590 this staircase in the basement has connected the kitchens and outhouses to the aristocratic apartments. The door at the end leads to a well which continues to provide spring water of great purity to the château.

23

A collection of Samuel Roger's antique fireplaces has taken up residence in the farmhouse.

23

Château de Larradé
Les Landes region

A Man of Taste

"My childhood was marked by the large houses owned by my grandfather and uncle, both headmasters. It was chance that guided my steps to Les Landes twenty years ago. I signed the bill of sale for the château on the corner of a table, happy as I was to finally own the family house that I had never had."

Gathered around a big table in the company of friends, basking in the shade of some ancient trees, Jean Mortier relates the story of Larradé, where he used to spend each summer. A new type of proprietor, Mortier is neither architect nor interior decorator, nor indeed does he conform to convention, but is rather a man of taste, cultivated and unpretentious. In buying Larradé he accepted it warts and all : its massive silhouette, its faults, its old furniture—right down to its tenant farmers. No question here of embarking on a massive renovation project. The first priority was to make the place comfortable, installing bathrooms and a heating system. The kitchen was relocated in the buildings formerly used for storing casks, adjacent to the house, necessitating roof repairs with the tiles that were on hand. The château's imposing location offers an exceptional view of the sloping vineyards of Chalosse, and, in fine weather, the Pyrenees can be seen in the distance. Orchard, garden, courtyard, and vegetable garden: all are harmoniously designed along the same lines, allowing a fluid concourse between each element of the building. The château is open to family and friends during the summer, and a themed ball is organized annually, to which the neighbors are also invited. Plays, shows, and "happenings" follow each other in quick succession. During a masked ball on the theme of animals, the walls of the courtyard were decorated with frescos painted by the guests ("That was before I redid all the façades!" says Jean Mortier). That same year a friend filled the swimming pool with hundreds of yellow plastic ducks. There are no holds barred when it comes to eccentricity.

Visiting the château is like reading a storybook: every room has a tale to tell. There is the ladies' boudoir, for instance, where an impressive gallery of worthies in their Sunday best line the walls; the priest's room, where prelates and abbots huddle around the huge fireplace; the gentlemen's dining room, festooned with their incarnadine portraits; the lady's bedroom with its tiny bed *à la polonaise*, decorated with a print by Françoise Subes, daughter-in-law to the decorator Raymond Subes, much in vogue in the 1940s, and the girls' and boys' dormitories, in which each toy has been lovingly acquired. On the side looking out over the farm, the traditional *sol*, or large common room, off which are found the guest rooms, has become a large curiosity shop, in which Jean Mortier has accumulated a collection of Victorian dioramas acquired in London. Stuffed animals and a hundred and one bits and bobs found in flea markets complete the picture in this unusual decor, which is at once droll, displayed to perfection, and above all unpretentious. "Jean is a bargain-hunter par excellence," enthuses one of his gallery owner friends, "he knows all the local flea markets and has impeccable taste. Visiting Larradé is magical." To be invited is a rare privilege.

———

Jean Mortier reveals the unique decor of his imposing castle, situated at the rural heart of the Landes region. A discreet patron of the local heritage and a passionate collector and bargain-hunter, he adores arranging his objects in such a way as to enable them to take part in a spectacle at once unusual, vivacious, and humorous.

———

The Story of Larradé

Thanks to an the discovery of an icehouse in the lower levels of the castle, it is possible to date its construction to the sixteenth century. Situated on a ridge and enjoying untrammeled views, it belonged to Simon de Larrey, Lord of Larradé. Two adjacent watermills irrigated the vineyards, which could also count on a large wash house (useful for cooling off) and a watercress bed, a great luxury for the period. A larger tower than the present one graced the castle at one point, as well as a bell tower whose component parts were discovered by Jean Mortier in the attic. It has since been restored and remounted, complete with bell, which tolls each dinner time. "Now everybody knows when we sit down to dinner!" laughs Jean. A wing reserved for tenant farmers is situated off the courtyard.

By dint of having being bought and sold several times, the castle had become a holiday home. When Jean Mortier bought it, the farm was no longer functioning. In addition to renovating the buildings according to the required norms, the gardens had to be reorganized, the vegetable patch cleaned up, and the panoramic views disencumbered. At this point a patch of dense grass was discovered at the base of the building. One of the elderly villagers revealed the existence to the owner of an icehouse and wash house at that very place. All hands were commandeered in a furious digging spree which eventually revealed these two rustic artifact in perfect condition: a minor miracle. Heavily involved as he is in the Foundation for the Heritage of Les Landes, Jean Mortier promotes the preservation of the region's historic buildings, such as the Chapel of Our Lady of Cyclists in Labastide-d'Armagnac, as well as the finishing workshop attached to the former forge at Brocas, "two projects that are close to the spirit of manual professions practiced at that time," as he points out. Thanks to his energy the gazebo at Portaou (see p.120) was allocated a subsidy from the first lottery to be earmarked for heritage, and the rose garden has just been opened to the public. "The cultural heritage of this region, for long hidden away, has been preserved, but many sites remain to be restored. It's high time they be discovered, now that the TGV has brought us so much closer to Paris."

31

29

The original natural bituminous limestone floor of the château's entrance, dating from the eighteenth century, is still extant. On a small console table in the shape of a half-moon under the staircase, we can see a curious shopfront sign featuring Napoleon's "little hat."

30–31

This large room in the old farmhouse contains the incredible collection of dioramas and stuffed animals that Jean Mortier acquired on bargain-hunting trips to London as well as in France.

32

A large coat of arms discovered in the Paris flea market now adorns the entrance to the former buildings used for storing casks.

33

The former kitchen, with its portraits of prelates and other ecclesiastical dignitaries, has been transformed into a "Bishops' Chamber."

33

34–35
The room referred to as "The Bishops' Chamber" has kept its original ocher-tinted walls. Items of furniture acquired in France and Spain have been placed around the huge fireplace, above which hangs a large *landaise* fabric originally used to protect cattle from heat and parasites. On the shelves stand lines of painstakingly collected old jars of preserves.

36
A mysterious ecclesiastical character stands guard between two doors.

37
Objects pile up unpretentiously in each room, in happy disarray.

37

38

38
Gentlemen decked out in their Sunday best cover the dining room's red walls, while numerous Delft plates adorn the mantelpiece.

39
The state-of-the-art kitchen in the former outhouses was inspired by that of Michel Guérard, a friend of Jean Mortier. The workbench, the central feature of the kitchen, was carved from one of the great plane trees in the garden.

40
A detail from the Great Blue Room, which has kept its 1950s printed fabric *toile de Jouy*, as well as its molded cupboards.

41
In this little room, referred to as the "mistress's bedroom," the bed *à la polonaise* is graced with a printed cotton bedspread made by Françoise Subes, daughter-in-law to wrought-iron artist Raymond Subes (1893–1970).

Château de Poncé
Loir Valley

The Art of Living

"At the time it was built in the sixteenth century, the staircase at Poncé provoked a shocked reaction. This was modern art! An enormous, seismic break in terms of style with all that had been imagined before," according to Guy de Malherbe. "In coming here, it seemed interesting to continue the element of surprise, and to invite art into our walls."

Passionate about contemporary art and the creative process, painter Guy de Malherbe and his gallery-owning wife Marie-Hélène de la Forest Divonne bought the Château de Poncé in 2010. Guy, a local, had visited this marvelous place several times, and it was here that he felt the first stirrings of art in his soul. He had never forgotten the famous Renaissance staircase, or the pottery workshop, in which he has since set up his easels. In this "oversized" secondary residence, historic reconstruction plays second violin to comfort.

"The enormity of the task discourages me at times," sighs Marie-Hélène de La Forest Divonne. "But arriving at Poncé I am carried away by the magic of the place and I tell myself that it's an adventure worth experiencing." The couple, who met as teenagers, "live" Poncé intensely and have swept up their three children and six grandchildren in the project. Here, artworks festoon the walls of the edifice, right up to the attic. Family furniture and collections of contemporary art jostle happily side-by-side in rooms whose ceilings are listed. Sometimes, at a turn in the corridor, you can spy a cradle or two, together with a pile of canvases waiting for the next exhibition. Poncé is no sanctuary, but a living house, open to family, friends, and artists alike.

The enormous demesne is also a non-stop construction site. The *Terrasse Caroline*, a three-story neo-Gothic folly in a state of collapse, requires complex restoration, for the tufa stone is fragile, and the cliff on which it is built is undermined by a vast network of tunnels rendering the structure vulnerable. The renovation of the nineteenth-century wing is about to be finished; bathrooms and heating have yet to be installed to make it comfortable. "When we bought Poncé," muses Guy de Malherbe, " there was nothing but water from the well to service our needs." Another major responsibility is the two-hectare garden, a listed monument, whose early sixteenth-century arbor in the form of a maze, as well as the symmetrical flower beds, require the presence of a full-time gardener.

In fine weather, the gardens and the extraordinary Renaissance staircase are open to the public, as are exhibitions in the outbuildings and art installations in the park, where important American collectors, fascinated by French heritage, are often to be seen criss-crossing its paths. Poncé also organizes splendid candlelit dinners surrounded by collections of contemporary art. On January 27, Feast of Saint Vincent, patron saint of wine-makers, the great covered guard room is turned into an annexe of the village fête, serving as the backdrop to mirthful, intimate festivities. A breath of fresh air for a heritage taken out of its museum-like context.

The château de Poncé, a little gem of architectural fantasy tucked away in the Valley of the Loir, never ceases to surprise. For the last ten years gallery owner Marie-Hélène de La Forest Divonne and painter Guy de Malherbe, in their quest to establish a dialogue between heritage and contemporary art, have carried on the tradition of overlapping different stylistic epochs.

The Story of Poncé

The fame of the Château de Poncé rests on its early sixteenth-century Renaissance staircase, whose six perfectly preserved vaulted ceilings are decorated with 136 caissons carved in tufa stone. Today, its owners have installed a part of their collection there, including paintings by Jean-Pierre Pincemin, Pierre de Buraglio, and Guy de Malherbe.

But something curious grabs our attention : this is the *Terrasse Caroline*, a gift from Amédéé de Nonant to his wife Caroline, built in Troubadour style, with the aim of keeping out prying eyes. This architectural folly, a romantic construction thirty meters high endowed with niches and orangeries, is currently being restored thanks to a grant from the *Mission Bern*. This is just as well, for part of the terrace constructed in tufa and brick had already collapsed.

It was on this bluff that the medieval castle once stood. However, during the Renaissance the owners saw fit to build a new château at a lower level, while at the same time laying out a vast pleasure garden, the maze of which is still to be seen. A dovecote was added in the seventeenth century, still perfectly preserved, and several outbuildings added in the eighteenth century now regularly house exhibitions. In the 1930s the new owner, a Doctor Latron, embarked on a huge restoration project with the intention of opening the château to the public.

Since the arrival of Guy de Malherbe and his wife Marie-Hélène, the Château de Poncé has once again become a private residence, although the staircase and gardens remain accessible to visitors; today, the château is a must-see for tourists visiting the Loir Valley.

48

49

47
The Renaissance château, built for Jean de Chambray around 1542, was graced with an additional wing in the nineteenth century, which we discover on arrival. A sculpture by Bernard Métais takes pride of place in the garden.

48
The fountain in the Italian garden, designed in 1930 by architect Paul Flandrin (1902–1936), son-in-law to Doctor Latron.

49
Partly collapsed, the imposing Terrasse Caroline is in need of major restoration. Embellished with several orangeries, it was built on the side of a cliff on top of the foundations of the former medieval castle.

50
One of the six archways of Poncé's wonderful Renaissance staircase, where works by contemporary artists are to be seen on each of the landings, such as this *Vanité au lambi* by Pierre Buraglio.

51
Homage to Pierre de Ronsard, whose birthplace, Couture-sur-Loir, near Poncé, is worth a detour: his manor house, La Possonnière, and its newly restored Renaissance gardens are open to visitors.

52

52
In Guy de Malherbe's studio we can admire paintings inspired by the cliffs at Étretat, which the writer Franck Maubert described thus in the preface to his monograph on the artist: "At the foot of the impregnable cliffs, you can feel the spray and the eddy of the artist's thoughts, a way of expressing eternity. It takes wisdom and folly to be a painter."

53
On the wall of a bedroom: a work by Alexandre Hollan.

54
One of the eighteenth-century bedrooms still has its listed wooden paneling; it is decorated with family furniture, such as this Louis XV escritoire.

55
This original wallpaper in one of the alcoves has been lovingly preserved.

58

56
The majestic Renaissance fireplace in the guard room is the only remaining vestige of the original castle.

57
Detail of a stained-glass window restored in the 1930s, in which a precious remnant of the sixteenth-century original has been reinserted.

58
Arcades connecting the Italian garden to the château's Great Park, listed as a *jardin remarquable.*

59
Perfectly preserved, the sixteenth-century dovecote contains 1,800 niches, while its rotating ladders are still in perfect condition.

Château de Lascours
Département du Gard

The Spirit of a Place

It was at the tender age of twelve that Pierre-Alain Challier made his first bid to the Prince of Croÿ. "I had dreamed since childhood of saving the little "Castelnau" buried in undergrowth, which I had discovered in the park of the Château de Lascours. I had emptied my piggy bank, thinking that the ruins would not cost much. The prince, who had never replied to my letter, bumped into me one day in a turn of the road. Brandishing his walking stick, he told me off, assuring me that his family had never sold anything, and never would."

During this period Bertrand de Latour used to draw sumptuous pictures of châteaux in his copy books, under the bemused eye of his teachers. The two aesthetes, destined to meet, now pursue a successful career in the arts. Pierre-Alain is the director of an eponymous gallery in the Haut Marais in Paris, while Bertrand is an auctioneer in Montpellier. In 2014, having overcome numerous obstacles, they bought the Château de Lascours.

Little did the Prince de Croÿ, the proprietor of this vast demesne situated between Anduze and Uzès in the Gard, think that one day the young dreamer from the neighboring village whom he occasionally bumped into in the château's undergrowth would one day achieve his goal. The prince, who had inherited the château in the 1970s, was unable to match the lavish lifestyle of his ancestors. The building was dismantled piecemeal under his very eyes by burglars, who systematically stole fireplaces and woodwork. The roof collapsed, the walls fell victim to damp. The sale itself, which dragged on and on, only accelerated the carnage. The die was cast on the day that the chapel's stained-glass windows disappeared. When Pierre-Alain Challier and Bertrand de Latour finally took possession of Lascours, their spirits were dampened immediately: "The day after signing for the château, we were all gathered for an impromptu meal in a room with a vaulted ceiling, when it began to rain," according to Bertrand. "There was water everywhere, forcing us to beat a retreat. Upshot: one hectare of roofing in need of urgent repair in order to save the edifice!"

Since then, a whole army of craftworkers as well as the Challier family have been busy on the construction site, for this mammoth project has turned into a big family adventure in which the talents of all have been mobilized. At first glance nothing appears to have changed, but with its new roof, English park cleared, and avenues recovered from the undergrowth, the château is almost habitable. No question of living there yet, but in summer, life goes on placidly in the "habitable" former kitchen with its minimum level of comfort. All the furnishings acquired through bargain-hunting over a long period have been accumulating in the store-rooms. The artworks, due to be exhibited in the future modern art foundation, are in boxes. The "artistic" phase will soon begin, to the great joy of the new owners of Lascours.

A childhood dream fulfilled, in which Pierre-Alain Challier and Bertrand de Latour continue weaving the thread of the tale of the château. Once the victim of constant pillage, this enormous estate close to the River Anduze is slowly coming back to life, thanks to the tenacity and fervor of its new owners.

The Story of Lascours

Lascours, meaning "there where the waters flow," was already a canal-irrigated demesne of some 500 hectares in the first century. The Gallo-Roman villa was transformed into a castle in the thirteenth century, crowned with the famous Tower of Valabiac, traces of which can still be made out. Following a period in the hands of monks, the castle became a seigneury owned by the powerful family of Bernard d'Anduze, Raimbaud de Sauve et Collias, which claimed a direct line to the barons of Lascours. The names—the Counts of Chaponay, the Princes of Croÿ—may have changed, but the line did not die out. Additions were made from the thirteenth to the twentieth centuries, money being no object until the 1930s. The "Castelnau" , the dream of the young Pierre-Alain, was a small castle built in the fifteenth century overlooking the surrounding vineyards; further on, the medieval fort and its keep became a *château de plaisance* whose main building was finished by General de Lascours, baron of the Empire during the Restoration. A vast body of neoclassical farmhouses as well as numerous outbuildings completes the picture.

The enormous English gardens have managed to preserve some of their more remarkable trees, including one spectacular plane tree sixty meters high. A hydraulic turbine was built in 1900 at huge cost in order to exploit the extraordinary network of canals, providing electricity for the château and its eighteen bathrooms. The stylistic labyrinth, which makes visiting Lascours today so fascinating, was a source of great irritation to one of the princes of Croÿ, who decided some time before WWI to demolish everything in order to build a new château, complete with pharaonic plans for the park. The outbreak of war, in which the prince participated, and later the Wall Street Crash in 1929, put paid to his dreams.

The last prince of Croÿ died childless in 2007 in his enormous, dilapidated château, which he left to his niece in South America. However, she found it impossible to manage the demesne. There was talk of it being converted into a hotel before it was finally bought by Pierre-Alain Challier and Bertrand de Latour. After two thousand years of war and the slings and arrows of fortune, the crippled château, sensitively restored by its new owners, can afford to lick its wounds.

66

67

65
Lascour's splendid façade, dating from the period of the Directory, has been endowed with a new roof. To the right, the medieval keep dominates the wonderful English park.

66
Lascour's owners have cleared one of the finest views of the park, which they will be soon able to admire from the future salon.

67
The "Chamber of the Survivors," as the owners have named it, houses a few traces of the château's finery, such as this mirror signed by artist Hubert Le Gall during his first visit in 2017. The mantelpiece, unfortunately, was ripped out by thieves.

68
The Prince de Croÿ lived in the south wing of the château until his death. The ground-floor apartments are furnished and offer a basic level of comfort.

69
The former kitchen in the south wing still functions, thanks to its 1930s oven. Glazed pottery acquired through bargain-hunting—as well as Anduze earthenware—has once again been pressed into service, until such time as it can be replaced.

74

70–71

The Princess of Croÿ's former bedroom will keep its alcove housing the bathroom, where a copper bath awaits installation. The ghosts of missing canvases haunt the vast room, shortly to be redecorated.

72

Situated in the medieval section of the château, this staircase leads to the former keep, the terrace of which is currently being renovated.

73

The small dining room of the *Old Lascours* is to retain its neoclassical decor as well as its original function. The new owners dream of having the nineteenth century wallpaper reprinted. A pleasing space, with a commanding view of the Great Terrace, dominating the entrance to the château.

74–75

The only piece of furniture to have survived successive thefts, the billiard table takes pride of place in the Great Salon of the *Old Lascours*, with its handsome eighteenth-century windows and timbered ceiling in French style, the beams of which were formerly painted. A portrait of Louis XVIII surveys the wreckage.

76

The Louis XVI fireplace situated in the enormous dining room of the *Old Lascours* has been ripped out, but one or two valuable Montpellier wall tiles dating from the eighteenth century have survived the carnage. These were inspired by Delft glazed earthenware but are decorated with *provençal* motifs. Pierre-Alain Challier and Bertrand de Latour are patiently hunting for bargains in order to restore the original mantelpiece.

77

At the angle of a corridor …

Château d'Écrainville

Normandy

All-Consuming Style

Always one step ahead of the rest, Arnold Van Geuns and Clemens Rameckers decided, at the beginning of the new century, to 'go green', long before 'neo-rural' became the rage.

"We had a small 'hut' near Étretat," says Clemens, "but we needed something bigger for work, and Paris was complicated. Then we found this château and our life changed. Owning a château bestows a certain chic, which is curious in this country of the French Revolution. But we're terribly handicapped in that we're not snobs! Now that we're the owners, we have the impression that we're constantly on stage, just like actors."

Although this inseparable Dutch couple insist that they are not typical château owners, they have slipped into the role with ease. From the time that they first met in the 1970s in the fashion department of the School of Fine Arts in Arnhem, these two artists, who have collaborated with the biggest names in the fashion industry, have shown that they have an innate sense of the theatrical. Lidewij Edelkoort, founder of the Trend Union Agency, who enjoys the reputation of being an oracle when it comes to what's "in," has said of them: "Their partnership, based as it is on mutual admiration of their talents, is unique … having left Paris for Normandy they have become trailblazers for the new rage for rural living, and have reinvented the countryside as if it were a fairy tale."

The extravagant decor of their château in Écrainville is a good example of their iconoclastic interpretation of history. Like Napoleon's architects Percier and Fontaine, they have created an ornamental style with its own unique language, where Louis XV slums it with the Empire, and where the languid aesthetic of the Pre-Raphaelites flirts with the stern lines of Bauhaus. In their unique pantheon, attention is drawn to their protean creations in an allegorical manner, in such a way as to be completely coherent. In the 1990s their first exhibition of decorative art, organized in 1991 by the Néotù Gallery in New York, was the talk of the town. They stamped their style on the collections of fabric, the art of entertaining and the furniture that followed. Thirty years on, certain fashion houses in search of inspiration continue to make use of their ornamental motifs.

In fact, they were before their time, and admit that lack of opportunities certainly hampered their career. Instead of being active in the leading fashion houses, the two young artists, newly arrived in Paris, preferred to spend their time exploring the labyrinths of the Louvre, the gardens at Versailles, and above all the refined decor of *Malmaison*. Educated as they were in the minimalist aesthetic of the Bauhaus school, they have never stopped marveling at the treasures of French heritage. Arnold, steeped in cultural history, has never tired of painting vast epic tableaux; he enjoys collecting dates of birth and death and placing kings and queens in hieratic frescos. Clémens, the more communicative of the pair, prepares their next museum exhibitions.

And so, in the priceless setting of Écrainville, the secret life of Ravage flows on.

Ravage, a pseudonym for Arnold Van Geuns and Clemens Rameckers, is a glimpse of pure fantasy on the coast of Normandy. A guided visit of the Château d'Écrainville, where these two designers are in the process of revolutionizing the decorative arts.

The Story of Écrainville

Attempting to tell the story of Écrainville resembles a police inquiry, since the château, which is not listed as a historical building, has no archives. Thanks to the interest in matters historical shown by the board of directors of the archives of the Départment de Seine-Maritime in Rouen, and notably Franck Descottes, the origins of the château are slowly revealing themselves. So it is that, looking through the archives pertaining to landed property, we learn that a certain Depardieu demolished his "house," destroyed by fire in 1884, and replaced it with a château, built in 1889. The new brick-and-stone construction in the style of Louis XIII was certainly inspired by the original seventeenth-century building. This large, landed property, endowed with 104 hectares surrounding the village, has left little trace of itself, but, according to legend, Depardieu introduced the young Guy de Maupassant to the Ministry of the Marine in Paris, and as result found him his first employment.

The famous Count Gaston de Pardieu is mentioned in the electoral register in 1924 at the time of the sale of the property to the Viscount of Reviers. Was the change of name a slip of the pen or does it bear witness to a ruse intended to enable escaping detection during the Terror? More research needs to be done to establish the provenance of the noble title. It has been established that the family or house of Pardieu d'Avremesnil was certainly an old noble Norman family, whose numerous descendants have, incidentally, succeeded in reconstructing the family tree back as far as 1250. It would seem that Depardieu is actually the Count de Pardieu.

The Viscount of Reviers lived peacefully in the château d'Écrainville until November 1944, at which point all of the archives were destroyed in what was described as "war action." Since arriving there, Arnold Van Geuns and Clemens Rameckers have discovered from older villagers that Écrainville had been requisitioned for the purposes of a military hospital by the Germans during WWII. On returning to her château in 1945, the Viscountess of Reviers suffered a major blow: the Germans had "massacred" her beloved château, and she refused to live there. The building remained empty until its sale in 1972. The new owner, who had made his fortune in the cosmetics industry, spent huge amounts on repairing the roof and transforming the interior according to contemporary taste, going as far as repainting it all in orange and yellow—floors included!

83
On entering the château, the visitor is confronted with two enormous Medici-style ceramic urns entitled respectively *Arrival* and *Departure*. They are unique, and hand painted by Ravage for the pottery works in Bavent, Normandy.
At the foot of the staircase are two bronze statues by Ravage, cast in the Fonderie d'art Bocquel (near Étretat), together with a statue of Joan of Arc acquired in the Paris flea market and repainted by its owners. In the background we can see a portrait of Napoleon shown in the 2010 *Ravage: Empires … et mieux!* exhibition at the Bibliothèque Marmottan in Boulogne-Billancourt.

84–85
The former dining room has gradually been transformed into a workshop. A forest seems to have taken root on the walls, inspired by the trees surrounding the château. Above each doorway can be seen an allegorical figure of one of the kings of France, in this case Charles X and Louis XVI.
To the right: *The fiancée of the Calabrian assassin*, by Arnold.

86–87
The doors opening out into the library are embellished with allegories of Prudence, Friendship, Misery, and Wealth, while on the ceiling, wallpaper designed by Ravage displays *trompe l'oeil* motifs.

88
Above the door to the dining room-cum-workshop stands a mosaic medallion by Bisazza, which incorporates motifs from the Napoleon IV dinner service designed by Ravage for Porcelaine de Paris.

89
An allegory of Henri IV stands above the dining room doors, whose wooden paneling is distinctly arboreal in tone.

90–91
Intended for a legendary Russian prince, the *Très russe* dinner service, entirely hand painted on fine porcelain and designed by Ravage, is unique. The supports were designed specially to accommodate the shape of the bowls and jugs displayed.

92–93

On the paneling of the music room can be seen several allegories relating to the horrors of war. Large portraits of wounded soldiers festoon the walls, reminiscent of the period during which the Château d'Écrainville was transformed into a military hospital. A kind of poor man's chandelier, a strange object made in Portugal out of recycled material, illuminates the room, with its armchairs upholstered by Ravage in hand-painted fabric. The tapestry entitled *Moorish head in the old style* was designed for Tisca.
On each side of the fireplace stands a plinth bearing a large glazed pottery vase in the "Solferino" style, designed by Ravage for the Faïencerie in Charolles.

94

In one of the bedrooms there is a series of thirty-two scenes, each describing a day in the life of Napoleon. They were exhibited in the Musée Bertrand de Châteauroux in 2009. The striped wallpaper was designed by Ravage and executed by Eijffinger. On the chest of drawers we see a plate created by Studio Job (Tilburg), whose designers are friends of the owners.

95

In the corner of one of the rooms there is a "ravaged" bust of Wagner.

Château de Ravel
Auvergne

Intimate Ravel

At the beginning of the twenty-first century lightning struck several times. The first was in 2014, when Joseph Achkar and Michel Charrière learned that their dream château was for sale. The second was a few months later, when the lightning set one of the wings of the building on fire. Four hundred square meters were destroyed. "A rare piece of luck!" insists Achkar, "because the fire revealed one of the most beautiful attributes of Ravel." This was Philippe le Bel's former chamber, now endowed with a wooden framework deliberately left visible, which has become an immense, perfectly proportioned room. "One can't just change a room's proportions," intones Joseph, on a tour of the château. The point was hammered home in the nineteenth century by Viollet-le-Duc: "One cannot remove part of a thirteenth-century edifice, or add decorative elements, without destroying its solidity and its very organism." "At Ravel, different epochs are piled on top of each other, just as they would be in an ordinary house," insists Michel Charrière.

Ravel is thus a construction site whose work is never done, evolving with each rebuild, and approved by the architects working for the Society for the Preservation of Architectural Heritage. So, for instance, dull paneling is capable of concealing a tangled, mysterious maze of corridors suddenly lit by a charming, tiny window, meaning that the original plans are turned on their head in order to integrate this new source of illumination into the decor. It's quite impossible to predict the flashes of inspiration displayed by the two interior design architects. "We like to invest each of our construction sites with poetry without repeating ourselves," insists Joseph, who refuses to be placed in a stylistic straitjacket.

Although Joseph Achkar and Michel Charrière have generously opened their château to the public, discretion is the name of the game. They have no website, nor are they to be found on social networks: their talents are communicated by word of mouth, attracting wealthy clients worldwide. Their indissoluble bond, forged in 1984, was serendipitous. For nothing, on the face of it, would have suggested an association between Joseph, a Lebanese graduate in law and political science, and Michel, a French architect educated at the School of Fine Arts in Clermont-Ferrand. Their partnership is built on the solid foundations of shared taste and style. "Beauty is not enough; it has to be right." Ever since the Center for National Monuments awarded them the contract to renovate the prestigious Hôtel de la Marine on the Place de la Concorde in Paris, they have been the center of attention.

"The fact that the Center for National Monuments granted us access to this prestigious building is proof that they finally trust us," says Achkar with humor. Interior decorators and compulsive collectors, the couple devour auction catalogs and feverishly hunt down tapestries and furniture dating from the Renaissance to the nineteenth century. They have also accumulated an impressive collection of wood paneling, which will have no trouble finding a home in the château's 7,500 square meters. They seem to derive pleasure from living in a huge building site: "This is a project that is going to help us grow old," says Michel Charrière with a wicked grin, hopping spryly over a pile of beams scattered in the middle of the Chamber of the States General.

The majestic castle of Ravel in the Auvergne has rediscovered its former luster. The celebrated interior designers Joseph Achkar and Michel Charrière reveal their talent for reinventing the past and blending different epochs with astonishing taste. Their restoration, at once historic and poetic, allows us to go back in time, as if in a dream.

The Story of Ravel

The imposing yellowish Castle of Ravel, something of a curiosity in this austere landscape of volcanic rock, comes as a surprise to anyone negotiating the leafy lane that is the *Allée du cabinet du loup*. In fact, the castle was constructed out of arkose sandstone, a robust, gold-flecked stone. Built in the twelfth century by the Lord of Ravel, the castle, dominating the blue hills of the Auvergne, was completed in the thirteenth century by Philippe le Hardi, who bequeathed it to his son Philippe le Bel. The solitary keep on the north façade was quickly supplemented with six more towers, connected to each other by constructions dating between the twelfth and fourteenth centuries, based on a more or less foursquare plan.

Ravel had been in the ownership of just three families before its acquisition by Achkar and Charrière. This was just as well, since it meant that it had been preserved from the ravages of destructive renovations. The château was bequeathed by Philippe le Bel to his advisor Pierre Flotte, France's first chancellor, and was handed on to Flotte's numerous descendants, the last of whom, the Estaing family, was wiped out in the Revolution. Charles de Riberolles became its owner in the early nineteenth century, and it was maintained by his family, who had it listed as a historic building, until the twenty-first century. When Joseph Achkar and Michel Charrière visited it for the first time, they were overwhelmed by the spectacular proportions of the thirteenth-century Chamber of the States General of Auvergne. This enormous room, containing heraldic friezes, had been partitioned off by a wooden enclosure concealing a strange ceiling decorated with grotesque characters, coats of arms, and fantastical beasts. "We were both immediately smitten by the potential of the place," say the two architects. What followed in terms of exploration was a series of dazzling discoveries.

Neither of them hesitated when it came to acquiring Ravel and its stock of furniture. Six years and one conflagration later, the living quarters have become habitable, the Chamber of the States General has seen its heraldic ceiling once more exposed to view, and the ancient living quarters of Philippe le Bel have risen from the ashes. Although the restoration of the Chamber of the States General has been finished, a great deal remains to be done on this enormous building site. New rooms are scheduled to be completed shortly, and a garden is shortlisted for planting. Visitors will have access to the château via a new entrance in the lower part of the great medieval walls, now transformed into exhibition spaces.

101
The austere east façade of Ravel, also known as the "oriental façade," is endowed with four towers, thus preserving its medieval aspect. It was also the side most vulnerable to attack, owing to the surrounding terrain. The foreground is dominated by the 23-meter high primitive keep, a vestige of the former castle. It juts out over the moats, once filled with water to repulse enemy attacks, and today refashioned as a large ornamental pond.

102–103
The huge landing on the first floor, the ceiling of which is decorated with coats of arms, leading off into the Genealogical Chamber, as well as the apartments converted in the seventeenth century by Admiral d'Estaing. The visitor is greeted by a portrait of a member of the Riberolles family and a collection of plaster busts dating from the seventeenth and eighteenth centuries, as well as from the Empire.

104
The former dining room is now a library. The impressive collection of engravings on its wall, featuring the ceilings of the Hall of Mirrors at Versailles, was commissioned by Louis XV.
The room opens out onto the Great Gallery, 22 meters in length, illuminated on the east side by tall windows looking out over Ravel's inner courtyard—something of a rarity in private French châteaux, which normally don't boast such large rooms.

105
The fireplace in the library was replaced in the eighteenth century by a stove.

106–107
In the *La Plaine* Room, with its breathtaking view of the Limagne and the volcanoes of the Auvergne, we see an eighteenth-century canvas depicting a scene from antiquity, which takes up an entire wall.

108
One of the bathrooms, complete with eighteenth-century bath in white marble.

109
The east-facing Alcove Bedroom, known as "Louis XIII's bedroom," is hung with flock velvet and decorated with seventeenth-century paneling.

110
The Insignia Room, formerly the guard room dating from the fifteenth century, features frescos of coats of arms, the majority of which are Auvergnois. They were restored in the nineteenth century. Its 200 square-meter floor in Ravel terracotta dating from the seventeenth century was restored in 2001.

111
Detail of an ebony cabinet dating from the reign of Louis XIII.

112
An Indian table inlaid with precious woods, complete with ivory legs, has been placed in the bathroom.

113
The walls in one of the south-facing rooms are entirely covered with medieval wall hangings of woven straw, used in the Renaissance period to insulate rooms from the cold. They were later covered over with tapestries with a view to completing the decor.

114

Detail of a sixteenth-century table illuminated by a thirteenth-century window (currently being restored) in Philippe le Bel's Great Chamber.

115

Philippe le Bel's former bedroom, complete with thirteenth-century fireplace, has become a large salon, the walls of which are covered with a collection of seventeenth-century tapestries. Two sconces dating from the early seventeenth century adorn a sixteenth-century wardrobe.

116

116
The King's Room, also known as the Gilded Room, in which Admiral d'Estaing was born, is noteworthy for its painted decor. The wooden chimney-piece boasts a canvas painted in 1655 by Isaac Moillon, a member of the Royal Academy. It features the kidnapping of Veturia, mother of Coriolanus, during the war between Rome and the Volsci.

117
The Great Room of the States General of the Auvergne, decorated in the late thirteenth century, is currently being restored. It boasts an imposing frieze representing the coats of arms of fifty French provinces. The room, the first example of heraldic decor to be found in France, boasts a remarkable ceiling of covered joists.

118
The bridge enclosing the château's courtyard, connecting the east-facing buildings to those facing west.

119
Stucco-embellished pillars are found between each window in the Great Gallery, adorned with medallions showing popular children's games: top-spinning, wrestling, kite-flying, and swinging.

LE POURTAOU DE JEAN RAMEAU
LES LANDES REGION

Cultural Heritage

A woman of the shadows, Jacqueline Sarthou became heiress to Jean Rameau through a combination of circumstances. She lives in *Le Portaou*, where the spirit of the poet, a native of Les Landes, haunts the humblest recesses of the great house. She dislikes exposing her house to the gaze of strangers, and to cross the threshold is no easy thing. "Everything I've done here is intended to preserve the poet's house, but I don't want to turn it into a museum for every Tom, Dick, and Harry."

And yet *Le Pourtaou* has had its share of misfortune: Jean Rameau's son Jean-Marcel was killed at the Battle of Verdun in WWI, and some time later his devoted wife Julia died of a broken heart, leaving him alone in the vast, memory-filled house. Rameau, reputed to be handsome, did not go unnoticed in the plush salons of the capital, where his amorous successes were not above inciting jealousy. An admirer of Victor Hugo, Rameau, born in 1858, shared the great poet's love of houses, art, and poetry. "My house is nothing more than a heap of dusty old mementos," he once proclaimed, with uncharacteristic modesty. For Rameau was an interior decorator before his time, constantly bargain-hunting, while pejoratively describing himself as *Drouoticus crepitans*; in fact, although eccentric and megalomaniac, he was extremely gifted. He made no bones about his admiration for the illustrious sources of his inspiration, Victor Hugo and Edmond Rostand, whose portraits hang in the library. The scene is set as soon as one enters the house, crossing the huge sol, which he referred to as the "great hall." He went as far as to describe its appearance in one of his poems:

> "The fireplace, where two lions gruff
> Dispense to th'intruder a welcome rough."

Jacqueline Sarthou, who spent her childhood and summer holidays in the house, became its owner in 2013. She occupies one wing and guards with jaundiced eye the remainder of the house, which has not changed an iota since Jean Rameau's death in 1942, as old postcards attest. Only the paintings, curtains and some armchairs have been permitted to be restored, thanks to the intervention of the local cultural affairs organization, or *DRAC*. Portraits and photos of Jean Rameau abound.

Jacqueline feels a unique bond with the spiritual father whom she never met, although her limitless admiration is coupled with a sense of irritation that she should have to manage this burdensome inheritance. The house would certainly have been earmarked for destruction, were it not for the aid of *Monuments Historiques*. Jean Rameau's immortality is assured and needs no help from the *Académie Française*.

Jacqueline Sarthou discreetly takes us on a visit of the writer Jean Rameau's unusual habitation. Rameau utterly transformed the property, a large farmhouse in the Landes, at the beginning of the last century. Now preserved as a treasure, the spirit of a now forgotten poet seems to hover over this strange and secretive sanctuary.

The Story of Pourtaou

When Jean Rameau bought *Le Pourtaou* in 1899, it was a large farmhouse typical of the Chalosse region. A cultured man of many talents, the poet prided himself on modifying its architecture in order to turn it into a château. He swiftly added a story with large openings and, on the west side, even designed the Italian terrace. This was quickly covered over since the clement climate of Italy is rather dissimilar to that of the Landes. And so, the lower portion of the house took on the aspect of a farmhouse, with its famous *sol*, an enormous room at the center of the building originally used to thresh corn and store tools. Jean Rameau immediately set about transforming it into an enormous reception room, about which he wrote the following verses:

> "The Great Chamber, interminably red.
> Red wall, red ceiling, bishops clad in red,
> And in the middle an enormous oak table, where the sculptor's chisel
> Carves in the wood's dense grain my head."

The poet furnished his property with items found through bargain-hunting and attending auctions. From the local clergy he bought tabernacles, Gothic rood screens, pillars, and statues of saints, which he cobbled together in order to create the strange neo-Gothic decor found in the bedrooms, in which he never forgot to slip a self-portrait disguised as a devil or a saint, or in a medallion.

In 1937 he sold *Le Portaou* as a life annuity to Jacqueline Sarthou's mother, who lived there following the poet's death in 1942. Her daughter Jacqueline, born four years later, spent all her summers there. After a long legal battle, she finally ended up in the house where she had grown up and decided to embark on a meticulous restoration.

Without the benevolent help of Alain Rieu, regional curator of the department of Historic Monuments in Bordeaux, who had the building inventoried, Jacqueline would never have managed its upkeep. The Society of the Friends of Jean Rameau, founded in 1993, aided the restoration. It also reprinted some of the poet's numerous literary works, of which there are fifty novels and 5,000 short stories. Thanks to the first heritage-designated lottery in 2018, the gazebo, under which Rameau is interred, could finally be restored. As for the newly replanted rose garden, we will have to wait a little before being able to visit it—in the future it will be open to the public from the month of May.

125

The "Theban Look" outbuilding used for storing casks in the former vineyard, which Jean Rameau had renovated in the style of the Directory, is topped off with an Italianate bell tower. Cornices and allegorical bas-reliefs modeled in cement are also his work.

126

The Great Chamber, 17 meters long, has kept its majestic table, under whose surface can be seen the famous effigy of Jean Rameau. At the far end of the room, we see the columns of an altarpiece acquired in Tartas, as well as large square vases and bas-reliefs adorning the imposing fireplace. Cabinet-maker Henri Cazaux restored and designed all of the furniture dreamt up by the poet.

127

At the main entrance to the Great Chamber, framed by numerous seventeenth-century paintings, we see a pediment decorated with a bas-relief in the style of Clodion. Above the fireplace of a second room there is a moving photographic portrait of Jean Rameau's wife and their son, who was leaving for the Front. They never saw him again.

128–129

"Behold the library in which, piled up opposite Apollo dozing on his lyre,
 Repose four thousand somnolent books—
 Which I have yet to read!"

This was Rameau's description of the library, painted in a subtle mustard-yellow (the original color), to which he added symbols: nine windows of nine windowpanes each, evoking the nine muses of the arts in Greek mythology. On the left we see a bust of Jean Rameau. Further on, a portico punctuated by three columns incorporates, at the level of the corbels, terracotta tiles designed by the poet, which feature the faces of loved ones. Three art nouveau circular portraits adorn the pediment. The chairs, in Empire style, and somewhat incongruously upholstered in *toile de Jouy*, have remained where Jean Rameau placed them.

130

Wanting to liven up the staircase, which he found rather boring, Jean Rameau invented a gallery of ancestral portraits, "to show the clothing and various finery with which humanity adorns itself throughout the ages." The series ends, in a touch of malicious humor, with his own portrait.

131

The "Emperors' Door," decorated with numerous allegorical scenes, opening out into the library with its delicately painted ceiling. The decor, all of which was conceived by the owner, consists of a lyre as well as medallions featuring Roman emperors and famous poets from Homer to Victor Hugo.

133

134

132–133
The baldaquin found in the bedroom referred to as "From the Good Lord" consists of columns taken from a late seventeenth-century altarpiece, as well as a high relief, and other items thought to have belonged to the church at Mouscardès. The bedside tables were formerly tabernacles.

134
The fireplace of this room is also composed of elements taken from an altarpiece. The ornamental chimney-piece, dating from 1900, was adapted in order to house a reliquary. The andirons, dating from the same year, probably come from Rameau's Paris apartment in the Étoile area.

135
Behind the post of an eighteenth-century processional dais turned into a sofa by Jean Rameau, we see a very beautiful Madonna (also eighteenth century), minus her rich attire.

135

CHÂTEAU D'OUTRELAISE

SWISS NORMANDY

Interior Scenes

Seduced by the charm of Outrelaise, Walid Akkad and Jean-Louis Mennesson have been its owners for some years now. The two designers share the same passion for this elegant château in the heart of Swiss Normandy, which has seen continual enlargement over the centuries.

Jean-Louis Mennesson styles himself as a "sort of scribbler" on his calling card, detesting to be categorized. Here, in the 2,500 square meters of his château, he runs no such risk as he passes from one studio to another: he has transformed several of them, and lives in each of them by turn, according to the season.

Walid Akkad, for his part, designs and makes jewelry in his enormous studio-cum-office overlooking the English garden. Nature and the precious stones with which he surrounds himself inspire the pure and sensual collections he creates for his Parisian gallery or for luxury brands. The garden is his domain. He is the one who created the vegetable garden and oversees the planting of the park.

Both owners grew up in large, child-festooned houses and adore welcoming their family and friends in a refined manner. The kitchen, open to casual visitors, prompts Mennesson to muse nostalgically on his grandmother's farmhouse in Picardy, with its château-like air, where about forty cousins would gather during the summer months. Each August 15 the children staged a big play. Walid thinks back to the elegance of the eighteenth-century Ottoman house that his family owned in Lebanon. It was precisely the ambience of their two respective houses that the couple wished to recreate. Their château's atmosphere can best be described as a theatre in which ephemeral plays are staged.

Outrelaise is a vast tableau, a series of rooms that reveal variegated decorative styles *ad infinitum*. Color is everywhere, the backdrop to a theatrical decor of historical grayish-blues juxtaposed with a perfectly controlled palette of intense hues. In this context unpretentious furniture is moved around, and the interiors, so Jean-Louis imagines, are in a constant state of flux. The library has been transformed into a concert hall, while the great Henry IV gallery takes on an enchanting allure on the occasion of dinners and other festive occasions. In fine weather, members of the Friends of Outrelaise can be seen in the gardens enjoying picnics.

Given its many decorative styles, Outrelaise is the dream setting for photo shoots commissioned by magazines or leading decorative brands. For many years camera crews were present within its walls, but successive crises have played havoc with an economic model constantly in need of reinvention.

"He who with himself would feel at ease / Should never leave Outrelaise," reads the inscription carved in letters of gold at the château's entrance. Walid Akkad and Jean-Louis Mennesson have no intention of leaving.

In the heart of Swiss Normandy, Jean-Louis Mennesson and Walid Akkad take us on a magical whirlwind tour of styles and epochs. A wonderful way to free oneself from the strictures of classicism through the use of theatrical artifice.

The Story of Outrelaise

The Château d'Outrelaise doesn't reveal all its charms in one go. The visitor needs to walk down a long avenue lined with 300-year-old plane trees in order to appreciate the superb Renaissance building.

Built by Gaspard Le Marchant, a wealthy heir and Advocate-General to the Court of Appeal in Normandy during the reigns of Henri III and Henri IV, this sumptuous property is situated in a large wooded demesne, through which flows the river Laize (hence the name Outrelaise), which has partly been transformed into a canal. Once past the statues of Vertumnus and Pomona, the gardens' tutelary deities, the château reveals itself.

The residence, built in the sixteenth century, has grown continually, notably with the addition in the eighteenth century of a wing in which the Marquise de Chambors established her salon, thus masking from Peeping Toms the north façade, built in 1604 in brick and stone in pure Henri IV style. This listed building recalls the layout of the *Place des Vosges* as well as that of the abbatial palace at Saint-Germain-des-Près, near Paris.

During the Romantic era Count Héracle de Polignac hit upon the idea of creating a park in the English style, which was designed by the Brothers Chatelain, and is currently open to visitors. A waterfall, small workshops, and some remarkable trees dot the walk, ending in an imposing dovecote peppered with niches in which pigeons can nest (sadly it was damaged during WWII). A delightful vegetable garden, designed and laid out at the beginning of this century, extends as far as the banks of the small canal.

Three decades have passed since Jean-Louis Mennesson and Walid Akkad have pooled their respective gifts, devoting themselves body and soul to the preservation, restoration, and refurbishment of their charming demesne.

142

141
The monumental entrance to Outrelaise, watched over by statues of Vertumnus and Pomona.

142
The much-damaged dovecote, constructed in the seventeenth century.

143
Peppered with niches for pigeons, the dovecote's carved walls are now home to a henhouse.

144
Two large wooden candelabra designed by interior decorator Christian Badin (1930–2019), as well as a Louis XVI painted wooden table, welcome the visitor in style.

145
Guest rooms lead off the first-floor wing, constructed in the eighteenth century.

146
The paneling of the corridor leading to the kitchen and office has been painted entirely in pink.

147
The refurbishment of the main kitchen, now in the former outbuildings, was the owners' idea. All of the furniture has been made to measure.

148
Walid Akkad's studio-cum-office in the small pavilion (an extension of the Henri IV arcade), furnished in the simple manner: we find a "Hudson" desk chair designed in 2000 for Emeco by Philippe Starck, a painting by Bernadette Kelly, and a bronze by Elisabeth Buffoli.

149
Work in progress on a jewelry collection.

150–151
"Scribbler" Jean-Louis Mennesson's "happy disarray," perched above Walid's desk.

152–153
Color is the name of the game in the owners' bedroom, which was originally three rooms; a bathroom, also painted mauve, is concealed behind the dressing room.

Château d'Agon
Near Mont-Saint-Michel

Sabine de Saint-Jorre and Jean-Michel Bourdon share the same passion for antiques. Their personal collection of family furniture and ethnic artifacts invites one to embark on a stationary journey on the Cotentin Estuary.

The Discreet Charm of Bourgeoisie

"When I was a child, I used to criss-cross the small villages of the Cotentin on a bike with my grandfather. Passing through the market town of Agon, my curiosity was piqued by its mysterious château, which I could just make out behind its high walls. I decided that I would live there one day." Sitting in front of the fireplace, Jean-Michel Bourdon relates the history of his beloved Château d'Agon, in which he has lived since 2005 with his wife Sabine de Saint-Jorre. In this part of the château, with its unorthodox layout, the couple are fond of welcoming friends and neighbors who drop in unannounced at teatime: the château's location, bang in the middle of the village, makes it an ideal place for the meeting of generations.

On the ground floor, kitchen, dining room and salon form a harmonious whole. In days past they were composed of reception rooms flanked on both sides by a ceremonial staircase, which has since disappeared. But it was the *piano nobile* that first impressed Sabine de Saint-Jorre. "I had no wish to leave our former house, an old farmhouse where I felt at home," she confesses, "but it was this imposing corridor that made me change my mind, as well as the magical view of the Sienne Estuary." Jean-Michel's office-cum-library under the eaves overlooks the misty, romantic coastline of the Channel, where, in good weather, one can make out the Chausey archipelago.

It is an ideal environment for housing the impressive collection of objects acquired by Sabine, a former antiques dealer, and Jean-Michel, former notary in Granville, who adopts a whimsical approach when it comes to making an inventory.

"Do you see that painting of a seascape above the door? It's worth absolutely nothing, but it was part of my childhood. It used to hang in the dining room of our old family home in Dinard. I was forbidden to talk at table, so, to pass the time, I used to look at the painting throughout the meal." Sabine, for her part, admits to having spent hours and hours in local thrift stores finding valueless objects, such as this imitation piece of Pont-au-Choux glazed earthenware—which she has placed in the kitchen—or certain purely decorative chipped plates, which are juxtaposed with priceless eighteenth-century glasswork.

"The house was begging to be taken," they say in awe, since all of their possessions feel at home there. This consists of a mixture of family furniture, some of which comes from the Château de la Mare, near Coutances (since demolished), which used to belong to the Annoville family. Scattered here and there in every room are a number of ethnic artworks which Jean-Michel inherited from his great-grandmother, who lived in French Equatorial Africa at the beginning of the twentieth century.

The charming mix set in train by the couple goes to make up a classic decor in which objects of interest are intertwined with holiday souvenirs, reminiscent of a fantasy world. You could say it's a somewhat eccentric family home, but not unnecessarily pretentious.

The Story of Agon

The first mention of the market town of Agon goes back to the eleventh century. The present-day château, whose oldest elements date back to the sixteenth century, recalls that distant era.

The medieval keep dominated the Estuary of the Sienne. Of this imposing construction only two truncated towers pierced with arrow slits survive, as well as a section of the crenelated wall that hugs the garden on the south side. The building constructed on its ruins in the sixteenth century rapidly became a holiday home, owing to its convenient proximity to the beach and market town.

Until the nineteenth century the sole owners of the château were the Guérin family. At a certain point it had belonged to the Villèle family, who owned large plantations in Réunion. The property was transformed and split up into smaller units with the passage of time, since the family produced only daughters. Today it is an ensemble of large attached houses complete with outbuildings, modified and enlarged during the eighteenth and nineteenth centuries in U-form and divided symmetrically down the middle. The austere granite-dressed north façade, with its air of a fortress, continues to impress. Prying eyes are kept out, thanks to high walls. The interior has been decorated with taste and has respected the original disposition of the rooms. The magnificent bicolored terracotta tiles in the kitchen and dining room come from the old keep, whose spirit is kept alive in the manor at Coutainville, situated on the outskirts of the village.

The grand staircase, which served all of the stories and was situated in the center of the château, was destroyed at the time the property was split in two, but one flight survived the disaster and is now a terrace at the far end of the Italian garden. Side stairs, located in the wings, have now replaced it. The building was lovingly restored in the twentieth century. The present owners have made no new additions apart from two bathrooms, and are in the process of restoring numerous annexes and living areas.

This truncated château is one of the hidden treasures of the narrow rue d'Agon, where it is surrounded by modest fishermen's cottages overlooking the estuary, the constantly changing nuances of which Barbey d'Aurevilly has described, in *Ce qui ne meurt pas (What Never Dies)*, as follows: "The very sky itself, this often gray and rainy western sky which penetrates our heart with its melancholy light, and, when we are far distant from it, fills us with nostalgia."

159
A family console table dating from Louis XIV's reign is flanked by two Louis XV chairs acquired through bargain-hunting, as well as a collection of Chinese porcelain, a blue Delft plate and a piece of eighteenth-century glazed earthenware. A portrait of Madame de Thieuville, painted in the eighteenth century, hangs on the wall.

160
The kitchen still has its superb patterned tiles. The furniture, designed by the owners, looks as if it has always been there. Various kitchen accessories line the shelves, acquired in local thrift stores and at flea markets.

161
In the linen room an old linen chest sits under a risqué engraving.

162–163

The centerpiece of this part of the château, the Great Gallery of the *piano nobile*, made an immediate impression on Sabine de Saint-Jorre. The long billiard bench upholstered in fake panther skin seems perfectly at home here. The walls are hung with valuable canvases from the family hoard, such as this Madonna and Child in the style of Pierre Mignard, while other paintings of negligible value add to the charm of the decor.

164

Designed by Jean-Michel Bourdon, the bathroom, formerly a bedroom, is structured around blue-painted partitions that conceal shower and toilet.

165

Between two wooden partitions we see a bath, while the walls are covered with engravings from the family collections.

166

A collection of engravings is visible above the fireplace, side by side with horse-jumping rosettes won by Paloma, the couple's granddaughter.

167

A printed textile, acquired in the Marché Saint-Pierre in Paris, adorns the walls and the headboard of the bed in Paloma's room. The wardrobes and paneling were all designed by Jean-Michel Bourdon.

167

CHÂTEAU DE FLÉCHÈRES
DOMBES REGION

Italian Allure

Fascinated by history, Pierre Almendros and Marc Simonet-Lenglart had been owners of the Château de Cormatin (a few miles north of the Taizé community) for fifteen years before deciding to make a detour to visit that of Fléchères, in order to see the set for the film *Diable par la queue*, directed by Philippe de Broca in 1968.

While there they bypassed the entrance and made a beeline for the park, which was covered in brambles. The imposing building, seen from that vantage point, exuded an atmosphere of poetry and mystery that they found overwhelming. It took them years to buy the property from the severely indebted owner. When they finally acquired it, the "sleeping beauty" had suffered two decades of abandonment and vandalism; it was completely gutted, and in a piteous state. Fortunately, its elevation to the status of listed building saved it from complete destruction.

Why own two châteaux when life would be simpler with just one? Almendros admits that embarking on such an adventure takes some doing. Their two solid, moat-protected castles are like protective bubbles that have helped them become reconciled with their chaotic childhoods. Their approach to the two properties, separated physically by a one-hour drive, is a purely individual affair. Simonet-Lenglart looks after Cormatin, while Almendros concerns himself with the restoration of Fléchères. A cultivated, discreet individual, Pierre Almendros has taken it upon himself to go it alone when it comes to the realization of certain of the projects. Thanks to the generosity of the fabric producers Verel de Belval and Prelle, several rooms have been renovated and are now open to the public. If summer visits have helped somewhat in balancing the books, a great deal of imagination is required when it comes to renovating each room.

"You make something more beautiful by avoiding the second-rate," wrote Daniel Boulanger, and Almendros has made it his credo, a kind of moral duty that has increased tenfold his determination to restore the extraordinary Ricchi frescos painted in the early 1630s. "The place swept us off our feet and allowed us to surpass ourselves," he whispers, as he looks at the works being restored. Coming across these rooms decorated by the Florentine artist, one is hard put to understand how the descendants of the distinguished Sève family saw fit to vandalize these masterpieces, covering them with paneling, plaster, and hideous wallpaper. The last of the line had reduced the property from 600 to 40 hectares, even going as far as to sell the well in the courtyard!

The new owners of Fléchères and Cormatin have no aristocratic titles and seek no riches. That said, they have devoted their entire lives and the fruit of their labors to heritage, and their greatest joy is to share that passion with visitors of every sort each summer; in so doing, they prove that nobility of heart is far more prestigious than a mere title.

The "Sleeping Beauty of La Dombes," rescued from destruction by Pierre Almendros and Marc Simonet-Lenglart, conceals marvelous frescos by Italian master Pietro Ricchi behind its honey-colored façade. The painter transports us on a journey into a seventeenth-century dream world of unimaginable beauty.

The Story of Fléchères

Since Roman times Fléchères has profited from its strategic location on the banks of the Saône. Its power increased with time, thanks to its proximity to Lyon. A castle was built there in the Middle Ages, the structure of which survived until the seventeenth century.

A tax collector and future provost for the merchants of Lyon, Jean Sève, Lord of Fromente and Villette, was one of the city's richest and most influential men at the turn of the seventeenth century. He seems to have played a key role in establishing the authority of Henry IV in 1594 following the Catholic League's five-year hold on power, setting him apart from his contemporaries. On acquiring Fléchères in 1606, he decided to keep the foundations of the thirteenth-century castle as well as its enormous moat, then built an immense three-story structure containing living quarters, flanked by two wings with apartments. Fléchères was the manifestation of the grandeur of the recently ennobled Sève family. This important example of domestic seventeenth-century architecture has barely changed since then.

Jean Sève died childless in 1631 and the barony of Fléchères passed to his cousin Mathieu de Sève, who at once set about converting and decorating the interior. According to the family legend, the Sève are direct descendants of the Marquis of Seva, a feudal dynasty from Piedmont whose records go back to the thirteenth century. As a means of establishing their prestigious and ancient antecedents, the Italian master Pietro Ricchi (1606–1675), at that time staying in Lyon, was commissioned to paint a series of frescos, on which he spent a year.

A family possession for three centuries, Fléchères was sold to a promoter in 1982 by the last of the line, Count Olivier de La Ferrière. Its elevation to listed building status in 1985 saved it from certain destruction, but the building, completely abandoned, had suffered (and still suffers) extensive damage.

Shortly after purchasing it in 1998, Almendros and Simonet-Lenglart discovered the priceless frescos hidden under eighteenth-century paneling, nineteenth-century plasterwork, and coats of paint dating from the second half of the twentieth century. They immediately set about their restoration. The frescos are to be seen in eight rooms, depicting in turn a military parade, hunting scenes, the Labors of Hercules, and architectural panoramas. It is one of the biggest works in its genre dating from the early seventeenth century still preserved in France. However, revelations continue apace, including the discovery of yet more frescos in a small chamber.

174

173
The outbuildings that partition off the château's courtyard comprise several structures, the roofs of which
have just been repaired.

174–175
The main staircase in Fléchères with its central void is one of the most remarkable attributes of the château,
and one of the oldest examples of its type in France. Decorated entirely with murals in the late seventeenth
century, it took its inspiration from Simon Vouet's decoration of Anne of Austria's apartments in the royal
palace.

176
The walls in one of the bedrooms had been covered over by a layer of plaster, completely masking these frescos representing a military parade given in honor of Henri IV's visit to Lyon in 1632, in which we can make out soldiers and dancers. At the far end of the bedroom a glimpse of another small room in the process of being restored: the wall had been chiseled before being coated with paint!

177
A series of painted rooms, which were once a study, an antechamber, and a wardrobe, now leading to Marc Simonet-Lenglart's living quarters.

178–179
A change of era in Marc Simonet-Lenglart's bedroom: he is among other things a connoisseur of decorative twentieth-century art. The walls, which are a similar red to Pietro Ricchi's frescos, are adorned with canvases by the Lyon artist André Fiol (1915–1999), painted between 1945 and 1960, as well as two academic works dating from 1910.

180
Pierre Almendros's summer quarters, furnished in a classical, eclectic style, with a mixture of works by André Fiol, 1950s furniture, and a bed *à la polonaise* draped with old fabrics acquired in Lyon.

181
An elegant clash of styles is the order of the day in the library, where we find an oil by André Fiol dated 1954, as well as two aquatints by Jean-François Janinet (1752–1814) featuring scenes from antiquity, after a work by Jean-Guillaume Moitte (1746–1810).

183

182

The Room of the Four Cardinal Virtues, decorated with *trompe l'œil* frescos, as well as an armchair created by the interior designer Jac

183

The frescos in the anteroom depicting the Labors of Hercules were found in a perfectly preserved state, thanks to having been covered over by paneling. In the opening of a doorway, we can glimpse the parade room where military tattoos took place.

184

The austere meeting room of the Consistory, or presbyterian council, where gatherings of local protestant families took place in the sixteenth century, has a view of the Fléchères garden. Embellished with pillars, it is currently being restored.

185

Enclosed by protective moats, the château is in constant need of restoration. The metal roof put in place in the nineteenth century in order to protect the two towers is due to be replaced by one of glazed tiles.

CHÂTEAU DE LA HAUTE BORDE
LOIRE VALLEY

Culture at Full Tilt

La Haute Borde, with its strange neo-Gothic façade, is sometimes the victim of snide remarks by purists, but the Barrère family immediately saw its potential when they bought it on a whim in 2007. Jacques Barrère, a major dealer in oriental art, and his wife Marie were passionate collectors, and their new second home would make a perfect setting in which to welcome the artists they cherished.

Nearly fifteen years on, their daughter Céline has taken over the running of the demesne. A young photographer with a very clear idea of what she wanted to do with this idiosyncratic property, Céline, together with two associates, Cécile Simon and Violette Platteau, embarked on a radical renovation of the building in order to create a meeting place for artists, friends, and casual visitors.

The former hotel-restaurant, with its indigestible-pastry-school style of architecture dating from the 1950s, was thought to be over the top. The notion of creating a locus of creativity in harmony with nature was born long before the Covid-19 crisis. The 2020 lockdown meant that the three associates—all in their thirties—could copper-fasten a project on which they had been working for two years. The renovation was undertaken by up-and-coming architectural bureau MPM Architecture, run by Charles Marmion and Jeanne Lefrand in Paris.

"We wanted to focus on environmentally friendly materials, both durable and recyclable, without compromising on luxury," explains Céline Barrère. The two architects have designed bathrooms in exposed brick and recycled marble for each of the bedrooms. The floors have been fabricated out of *cocciopesto*, a mixture of crushed brick, crushed marble, chalk, and cement. The wing reserved for artists has been conceived along the same simple, monastic lines, with its broad corridor off which are situated the bedrooms. On the ground floor, the reception areas, repainted from top to bottom in white, have been stripped down to a bare minimum.

Céline Barrère, growing up as she did surrounded by works of art, drew on family collections of furniture constructed by important twentieth-century designers, as well as the oriental art that she adores. Other elements in the decor were acquired in Northern Europe with the help of stylist Erin Korus and antique dealer Julie Barrau. "We were impressed with the result," enthuse Jacques and Marie Barrère. "With their modern touches, Céline and her friends have breathed new life into La Haute Borde. It's a living place, creative, at one with its epoch: a true success."

A succession of musicians, visual artists, writers, and casual visitors has turned up since the official opening in the summer of 2020. Antoine Carbonne, at the time exhibiting at the Villa Noailles Museum (near Hyères, on the Côte d'Azur), was among the first of the invited artists; he has painted a large fresco surrounding the fireplace in the living room. The farmhouse, situated on the far side of the road, hosts several spaces conducive to creativity, including a pottery workshop. The permaculture vegetable garden has already produced its first harvest, used by the young chefs regularly invited to La Haute Borde's enormous kitchen. Utopia has become reality.

Situated in the heart of the Loire valley, the Château de la Haute Borde has just had the finishing touches put to its transformation into an artists' residence. A place open to art and nature, it is conceived as a huge workshop intended to give free rein to inspiration.

189

The Story of La Haute Borde

Constructed in 1816 at Rilly-sur-Loire by the Boisredon family, the Château de la Haute Borde dominates—and will continue to dominate for several decades to come—a large rural property endowed with several farms.

Berthe Jousselin, a wealthy young widow, bought the property from the Countess of Boisredon in the late nineteenth century, with the aim of transforming it into a locus for culture; a talented musician and singer, she was also a woman of taste. Feeling somewhat hemmed in by the château, she enlarged it, adding a large reception salon and a terrace giving on to the park. In 1925 she married Prince Korewo, a young and penniless Russian aristocratic émigré.

Berthe de Korewo, surrounded by this pastiche neo-Gothic architecture with its trappings of theatrical decor, hosted numerous *soirées*. On her death in 1946 part of her collection was donated to the Museum of the Château de Blois. La Haute Borde, sold in return for a life annuity, was transformed into a hotel-restaurant in the 1950s.

Although the Château had enjoyed a certain prestige for fifty years or so, it had also suffered from numerous less-than-happy modifications. Having often stayed there by the time they acquired it in 2007, the Barrère family knew it well. The old-fashioned decor was modernized, only the kitchen remaining in its original state. As collectors of oriental art, they were not interested in historic reconstruction as such: their concern was to brighten up the space available, by means of pruning and clearance, in order to exhibit their collection and invite family and artist friends. When the day-to-day running of the château was taken over by their daughter Céline and her friends, Céline transformed it into an artists' residence. The fact that a younger generation has breathed new life into a place that has long been devoted to the arts cannot but please this family of aesthetes.

191
At day's end: Haute Borde's pristine façade, bathed in a delicate pink.

192
On entering, the visitor is greeted by a desk designed by Jean Royère (1902–1981) and a chair by Francis Jourdain (1902–1981), dating from the 1930s.

193
The large leather sofa created by Dutch designer Martin Visser (1922–2009), placed in front of the fireplace next to a Francis Jourdain armchair. The château's paneling and fireplace are both painted entirely in white in order to highlight the works on show.

194–195
The kitchens in the former restaurant have taken on a new lease of life thanks to the young chefs living in the château. The organization of gala weekends of "taste, style, and revelation," open to the public by reservation, is now possible.

196

A masterly touch on the part of MPM Architecture: the bathrooms are a combination of exposed brick and Italian marble offcuts.

197

All of the furniture in the bedrooms has been made to measure from spruce and can be disassembled with a view to potential recycling. Wang Keping's sculptures have been repurposed as bedside tables.

198

Designed by MPM Architecture, the swimming pool is in concrete aggregate. Its pool house in untreated concrete is home to a stainless-steel furniture unit.

199

The château's enormous pond forms the starting point for reverie and soul-searching.

MANOIR DE LA CARLIÈRE
IN THE HEART OF NORMANDY

À la British

Renowned decorative artist Michelle Halard makes no excuses for the decor of *La Carlière*. In this small Norman château, "Verdure," a term for tapestry with trees as principal motifs, doesn't necessarily refer to "tapestry," but also to textiles, cushions, and rugs. Books are piled up on tables, and plush sofas are a temptation to laziness.

This elegant, perfectly proportioned seventeenth-century manor immediately made an impression on fashion artist Peter Copping, the first to visit it twelve years ago. His companion Rambert Rigaud, on discovering its charms, felt exactly the same. At first it was a holiday residence, stuffed with bric-a-brac, in which they stayed during weekends and holidays before settling down to a long period of renovation. And renovation there certainly was: the roof, the spartan bathrooms, and the dilapidated kitchen all needed a complete revamp.

Peter Copping, originally from Oxford, was educated at St Martin's School and The Royal College of Art. Today, he collaborates with the big names in the fashion industry. Although fashion is his universe, he is no stranger to the world of decoration. One day, while giving a helping hand to the scenographers in the Conran Shop, he bumped into Christian Lacroix. The opportunity to introduce himself was too good to be missed. From then until the end of his studies, he attended several of Lacroix's masterclasses in the designer's haute couture atelier. On graduation he went to Italy, and when he returned to Paris he studied with designer Sonia Rykiel. Both of these designers, who are passionate about the decorative arts, certainly informed Peter's aesthetic palette. Peter has the rare talent of being able to combine prints with color in an unpretentious style, which Rambert Rigaud tempers with a decidedly French taste. Both of them laugh this off: "We are not interior decorative artists, in fact we come from very different backgrounds, but our aesthetic views complement each other. You could say it clicks!"

Rambert Rigaud, educated at the Employer's Federation School of *Haute Couture* in Paris, has been in charge of several fashion studios, including the John Galliano studio (with Dior), the Stefano Pilati studio (with Yves Saint Laurent), as well as that of Marc Jacobs and, currently, Balenciaga. At the age of forty, exhausted by the fashion collections, he stopped everything and became a florist. For a period of two years he successfully ran a florist's store in the *rue de l'Université* in Paris, being commissioned as a scenographer for fashion shows and private events—a fruitful interlude. This was followed by a two-year stint in New York, where Peter joined Oscar de la Renta's team. On their return, the couple decided to make *La Carlière* their principal residence. Furniture and other objects, patiently acquired over the years, were finally taken out of storage. Peter is a regular at auction houses, while Rambert prefers visiting the local antique dealers and flea markets. Their combined whims go to make up a very personal decor, in which English style, somewhat eccentric, merges with that of a more gentrified French style. Here, for instance, we find a gentleman's bedroom painted in porphyry pink, furnished in the Empire style. A little further on we come across a bathroom decked out in arsenic turquoise. The couple's manor personifies, like their couture, a very Parisian style, which fits them like a glove, and which has been defined by Louise de Vilmorin in *La Couture à Paris ou le gout de l'idéal* as "perhaps miraculous, this penchant for the ideal, this taste for risk-taking, for embracing challenges—in short, a feeling that time itself has been thrown into disarray."

In the heart of Normandy, fashion artists Peter Copping and Rambert Rigaud demonstrate their know-how when it comes to style, while at the same time ignoring convention. We're going to explore their seventeenth-century country house with its cottage-like flavor.

The Story of La Carlière

Few documents survive that could enable us to trace with any accuracy the history of *La Carlière*. Any research leads to a dead end, the more so since the building is not listed. The fief formerly belonged to Squire Guillaume Rogier, who is mentioned in the context of the château's sale as being an annuity to the village curate by the squire's widow, Isabeau de Rochefort, lady of La Carlière, in 1509. In 1558 Marie, daughter of Guillaume Boessel, lord of La Carlière and Tandelais, married François de Gibot, squire to Madame d'Angoulême, daughter of Francois I. Francois de Gibot became Lord of La Carlière in 1579. The property remained in this noble Angers family of ancient stock until the beginning of the eighteenth century.

The Château de La Carlière was built after the Thirty Years War, which wreaked havoc in Europe from 1618–48. It is thought that one of the Gibot family financed its construction. Its architecture, featuring a central portion extended by two wings, is particularly harmonious. The north front features a circular turret graced with a tapering, conical roof that dominates the surrounding countryside. The staircase it houses serves every floor and is in perfect condition. Likewise, a stone fireplace still exists in the dining room on the ground floor. Some windows have been added to the north-facing part of the building, and a terrace added in the eighteenth century gives direct access to the garden from the reception area. A farmhouse and its outbuildings can be seen in the fields surrounding the demesne.

In 1792 *La Carlière* was sold to Jeanne Marie Castaing, who married Esmée Augustin Frécot Saint-Edmé the following year. The couple transformed the garden, until then adjoining the farmyard, into a pleasure park.

Frécot Saint-Edmé, deputy judge of the civil court in Alençon and mayor of the local village between 1805 and 1815, had been smitten by the poetry bug, and was something of an expert in Latin. He embarked on a translation of Virgil and published the poems anonymously in a collection entitled *L'Énéide de Publ. Virgile, en vers français*. He was lambasted by the literary critic Léon de La Sicotière, who described Saint-Edmé's work as being a travesty of Virgil, cruelly citing certain passages:

> "As far as her waist she had the happy aspect
> Of a young beauty; the rest of her body
> Resembled that of a blue whale:
> Her belly that of a wolf, her tail that of a dolphin."

The book caused such a literary scandal that is was removed from circulation, and today no trace of it can be found. The misunderstood genius died in his manor in 1825.

Since the end of the nineteenth century *La Carlière*, which has lost all its agricultural land, changed owner several times, until Peter Copping and Rambert Rigaud acquired it in 2009 and undertook its restoration.

206

205
Euphorbias planted by Rambert Rigaud add a touch of springtime color to one of the walled gardens.

206
Charming pathways connect the individual gardens.

207
The former small kitchen is now a dining room boasting a table once belonging to a monastery, acquired in the Paris flea market, as well as chairs bargain-hunted in Scotland. Similar in aspect to an alcove, it opens out into a new room, recovered from the outbuildings.

208
Detail of a sofa upholstered in striped fabric in the Winter Room, part of the Madeleine Castaing collection (edited by Edmond Petit).

209
Detail of a Victorian pedestal table covered with a design in petit point.

211

210–211
The library in the Winter Room, made to measure and painted in black, plays second fiddle to the superb Robert Kime sofas upholstered in striped fabric, whose cushions were re-covered by Peter and Rambert. It took ten years to complete the decor with objects patiently acquired through antique dealers.

212
In Peter Copping's study-workshop, bargain-hunted objects rub shoulders with contemporary art, such as this study in green and blue by Marek Halter, placed in front of the fireplace.

213
Rambert Rigaud is fond of picking flowers from the garden in order to make bouquets (replenished each day), which he places strategically in each of the rooms.

214
One of the bedrooms, painted in Farrow & Ball's daring "Porphyry Pink." The four-poster bed is decorated with a printed fabric designed by Robert Kime for Chelsea Textiles. The Louis XVI secretary belonged to the Rambert family.

215
In one of the bathrooms decorated with Lewis & Wood wallpaper, the bath is surmounted by a chimney-piece dating from the Directory period, bought in an auction house in Alençon. The chair, acquired from a bric-a-brac trader by Peter, has been embellished with *trompe l'oeil* marble.

CHÂTEAU DE DIGOINE
BURGUNDY REGION

The Never-Ending Story

Remilleux is a lucky man. A former journalist who currently produces the TV program *Secrets d'Histoire*, he explains his success as follows: Before buying Digoine in 2012, he had owned the Château de Groussay (just west of Versailles), the celebrated residence of Charles de Beistegui, which he sold after ten years of passionate loving care. In order to be able to afford Groussay he had sold a small eighteenth-century house in the Berry region. He started from nothing—but not everything can be explained by chance.

A great lover of decorative art, whose expertise and aesthetic make him the envy of his profession, he is a prudent collector whose taste was formed at a very early age in the flea markets of Paris and London, as well as in auction houses. "I've done the only thing I know how to do: please myself," he explains by way of justification, accusing himself of a bulimic urge to acquire the inordinate number of books, items of furniture and works of art that surround him. Jean-Louis Remilleux has found in the Château de Digoine an endless playground, endowed with hundreds of hectares of land, a pond, and several outbuildings, which he is restoring with gusto.

But this is a man for whom nothing is set in aspic. In September 2015 he sold off part of Digoine's furnishings to Christie's. "When I run out of space, I sell something off. Rather like being at the casino, where you cash in your chips and leave. I am fond of my possessions, but they are not human: they remain objects."

Within five years the empty spaces left by these sales have already been filled up again. The decor of each room is executed with exquisite taste, the fruit of feverish trips to antique shops, or the painstaking study of auction house catalogs. Remilleux never tires of telling the story of his finds; to follow him through the maze of his château is to be guaranteed protection against boredom.

Every piece of furniture, every painting and every ornament provides the backdrop to an enthusiastic digression, peppered with hilarious anecdotes that cannot fail to amuse the listener. A natural storyteller, he considers himself both lucky and lazy, but is a man of true culture notwithstanding, combined with a strong will. "Ornaments, whether taken separately or together, besides the fact that they are poems, are a way for the connoisseur to express himself in secret, to whisper secrets to all and sundry," as Paul Morand aptly puts it in *L'Enfant de cent ans*. Jean-Louis Remilleux's residence is far more than a pretty interior.

Everything had to be started from scratch in the case of Digoine; fortunately, the sale of Groussay, coming as it did as a sort of miraculous manna from heaven, rendered the task that much easier. "I've been here ten years now; who knows, perhaps one day I'll grow tired of it. People are prisoners of family ties. As for me, I didn't inherit a château and can sell it if the fancy takes me. I like to vary my pleasures."

A diversionary tactic? It's difficult to imagine Jean-Louis Remilleux abandoning the peaceful Charolais-Brionne countryside …

From the moment that Jean-Louis Remilleux took in hand the extraordinary feat implied in its preservation, Digoine, nestling in its vast Burgundian demesne, can once again reveal its splendor. The château invites us to take a nostalgia-free deluxe promenade through the universe of this captivating art collector.

219

The Story of Digoine

The lords of Digoine had owned the terrain that bears their name since the eleventh century. Following the marriage of Marie de Digoine to Robert de Damas, the ancient medieval castle began to take on the aspect we recognize today. The Damas of Digoine thought big: the construction had to be rock solid. Two imposing towers protected the north façade, while two others were constructed at the end of the south esplanade, enclosed by dry moats.

When the wealthy Reclesne family bought the demesne in the eighteenth century, the castle was turned into a *château de plaisance*. Transformations, in which architect Edme Verniquet played a key role from 1750 on, lasted fifty years. The founder of the School of Fine Arts in Dijon and a friend of Buffon, Verniquet had participated in the laying out of the *Jardin des Plantes* in Paris, as well as designing several imposing townhouses in the capital.

Throughout his career the architect was responsible for designing a dozen or so châteaux in his native Burgundy, including that of Digoine. Under his supervision the austere north façade was endowed with a double colonnaded portico, a pilastered top floor surmounted with a carved trophy (in the eighteenth century the term "trophy" referred to military exploits), and superb wrought-iron balconies. The metamorphosis reached its apotheosis with the entrance to the south façade, adorned with two high French windows and a neoclassical pediment. The two medieval towers surrounding the new construction were graced with lantern domes.

The first half of the nineteenth century saw Digoine at its most splendid. Its new owners, Count Aimé de Chabrillan, chamberlain to Napoleon, and Countess Zéphyrine Olympe de Choiseul Gouffier, heiress of Digoine, continued the transformation, adding a heated greenhouse, a library and a small theatre in which Jacques Offenbach and Sarah Bernhardt performed. The count, whom Remilleux nicknames "Le Beistegui de Digoine," had benches installed in the vestibule, bas-reliefs, and consoles supported by legs carved in the shape of lions' paws, designed by Clodion, which the Count had inherited: they came from the monumental nymphaeum of the *Hôtel de Besenval* (now the Swiss Embassy) in Paris.

Digoine was sold in 1908 to the Marquis de Croix, who bequeathed it to his descendants. When Remilleux bought the château in 2012, it was empty. However, he succeeded in buying some of its furniture during a large auction organized by auctioneers Beaussant-Lefèvre. Having made further improvements with the help of pieces from his own collection, he embarked on an enormous restoration: floors, paintwork, roof repairs, electricity, and the installation of cast-iron radiators. An additional, prestigious project is on the horizon: the restoration of the small amateur theatre, designed in 1842.

221
The greenhouse adjoining the château, commissioned by Chabrillan in 1830.

222
Restored in 2008, the greenhouse is now home to Jean-Louis Remilleux's collection of plants, including several agaves that he brought back from Sicily—a reminder of his palace in Noto.

223
Detail of the greenhouse's neoclassical façade.

224
The Great Salon, perfectly aligned with the château's majestic entrance.

225
The south-facing Winter Dining Room is graced with a large portrait of *Zéphyrine Olympe de Choiseul Gouffier, comtesse de Moreton Chabrillan* (1782–1828) painted by Jean-Baptiste Paulin Guérin in 1823. In the foreground we see two stone consoles in Tonnerre stone with their characteristic lion's paw feet, which once graced the nymphaeum of the Hôtel Besenval in Paris (today the Swiss embassy), as well as bas-relief casts (also by Clodion), the originals of which are to be found in the Louvre.

226

The Great Salon has beautiful views of the garden-level ceremonial rooms. The architraves above the doors, executed in grisaille, are perfectly preserved. A ceramic vase by Théodore Deck (1823–1891) is a nod to its neighbor, which dates from the Second Empire. A collection of ornithological plates manufactured by Darte can be seen on the console table.

227

The fireplace in the Great Salon is surmounted by a Louis XVI clock and two portraits of the Mademoiselles de Blois and de Nantes, two of the daughters born to Louis XIV and Madame de Montespan.

228–229

The north-facing Summer Dining Room, also referred to as the Buffet Room, is equipped with two devices for reheating and cooling dating from the eighteenth century, which did service for both dining rooms. On the table can be seen a spectacular *Temple of Love* in bisque porcelain, a present from Napoleon to the Empress Marie-Louise.

230

Jean-Louis Remilleux never parts company with these two jealously guarded ceramic baboons placed on the mantelpiece of the small green drawing room-cum-library. The clock, acquired in the Portobello Road flea market in London, also has sentimental value. A portrait of the Duchess of Bourbon (Mademoiselle de Nantes, daughter of Madame de Montespan and Louis XIV) in mourning hangs on the wall.

231

A view of the Card Room with the 'last' two (stuffed) wolves of the region.

233

232
The neo-Gothic rotunda-shaped library, commissioned by the Count de Chabrillan in 1830.

233
At its most spectacular during sunset, this engraving-lined corridor is furnished with a Russian bench acquired during the furniture auction of fashion designer Karl Lagerfeld (1933–2019).

234–35
The bed of Madame Roland, a society lady guillotined in 1793, entirely restored in a silk workshop in Prelle by the Burgundian tapestry artist Beccat. A medley of vases can be seen on the mantelpiece, together with some Louis XVI perfume-burners.

234

236

236–237
The soon-to-be-renovated tiny amateur theatre, whose curtain and decorations were painted by Pierre-Luc-Charles Ciceri (1782–1868), chief scenographer at the Opéra in Paris. He had considerable influence on the development of scenography during the first half of the nineteenth century.

List of Addresses

• Château d'Outrelaise
14680 Gouvix
Park and gardens open to the public
from June 15 to September 15.
www.outrelaise.com

• Château d'Écrainville
Ravage
Instagram @ravageart

• Château de Ravel
63190 Ravel
Guided visits during the summer
months.
www.chateauderavel.com

• Château de Poncé
72340 Loir-en-Vallée
The gardens and Renaissance staircase
are open to the public.
There are exhibitions in the outbuildings and in the park.
www.chateaudeponce.com

• Le Pourtaou de Jean Rameau
3036, route du Pourtaou,
40300 Cauneille
The Rose Garden is open to the
public from May 1 to July 15.
roseraiedupourtaou.fr

• Château de Marcellus
47200 Marcellus
Origines: Architecture & Heritage by
Samuel Roger.
Space available for rental.
www.origines.fr

• Château de la Haute Borde
6, la Haute Borde,
41150 Rilly-sur-Loire
Artists' residence and guest rooms.
www.c-h-b.fr

• Château de Fléchères
01480 Fareins
Guided visits of the château and
gardens.
chateaudeflecheres.com

• Château de Digoine
71430 Palinges
Open to visitors from April to
October.
chateaudedigoine.fr

Sources

REFERENCE WORKS

Barbey d'Aurevilly, Jules,
Ce qui ne meurt pas, 1884, Paris,
Honoré Champion,
"Textes de littérature moderne et
contemporaine," Band 4, 2015.

Bedel, Jean,
*Les 1 000 Questions sur les antiquités,
l'art, la brocante*, Paris, Hachette,
"Les 1 000," 1992.

Canovas, Manuel,
Le Guide des tissus d'ameublement,
Paris, Hachette,
"Les Grands du style," 1986.

*Création en France. Arts décoratifs
1945–1965*, Montreuil,
Gourcuff Gradenigo, 2009.

Janneau, Guillaume,
Dictionnaire des termes d'art,
Paris, Garnier, 1980.

La Sicotière, Léon de,
*Deux poètes excentriques.
L'abbé Gérard Des Rivières,
Frécot Saint-Edme*,
1885–1895, Paris, Hachette Livre,
BNF, 2016.

Morand, Paul,
Rococo, 1933, Paris, Grasset,
"Les Cahiers rouges," 2006.

Rameau, Jean,
Songes d'un poète, publiyhed by
l'Association Les Amis
de Jean Rameau, Orthez,
Louis Rabier, 2015.

Ravage and Bak, Saskia,
Ravage. Illustre inconnu, Eindhoven,
Lecturis, 2017.

Reyniès, Nicole de,
Le Mobilier domestique, volumes 1
and 2, Paris, Imprimerie nationale,
"Principes d'analyse scientifique,"
1987.

Riegl, Aloïs,
Questions de style, 1893, Paris, Hazan,
"Collection 35–37", 2002.

Rubisiak, Nicolas,
"Manoir de Larradé. 1254–1871"
(recherches historiques).

Vasseur, Sébastien,
"Le Château de Fléchères: état des
connaissances actuelles sur un fleuron
du patrimoine," *Dix-septième siècle*,
2005, 3, n° 228, S. 547–562.

Vilmorin, Louise de,
Articles de mode, Paris,
Le Promeneur, 2000.

Viollet-le-Duc, Eugène,
Entretiens sur l'architecture, 1863,
facsimilé, Bruxelles, Pierre Mardaga,
1977.

OTHER REFERENCE WORKS

Base Mérimée
(www.poS.culture.gouv.fr):
POP, or platform for open discussion
about heritage.

Persée (info.persee.fr):
has as its objective the promotion of
documented heritage.

Pôle des archives historiques
de la Seine-Maritime, Rouen.

Acknowledgements

We would like to thank those featured
in this book who generously shared
with us the daily life of their châteaux
during our research:

Gilles Valette and his daughter
Jeanne, who designed the layout of
our châteaux reveries, and

Véronique Lopez and Christian
Tourret, without whose aid this
project would not have been possible.

We would also like to thank Yves
Badetz, Sylvie de Chirée, Franck
Descottes, Alix de Dives, Nicolas
Mathéus, Brigitte de Malau, and
Philippe Sinceux.

TABLE OF CONTENTS

239

First published in French under the title *Châteaux et Dépendances* by Éditions de La Martinière, 57 rue Gaston Tessier, 75019 Paris, © 2021.

© 2022 Prestel Verlag, Munich · London · New York,
A Member of Penguin Random House Verlagsgruppe GmbH,
Neumarkter Strasse 28, 81673 Munich

A Library of Congress Control Number is available. This book is available from the British Library.

Front and back cover photographs: Marie Pierre Morel

Editorial Direction: Sabine Schmid
Translation from French: Conor Biggs
Proofreading: Fiona Biggs
Copy-editing, Typesetting: Print Company, Vienna
Layout: Gilles and Jeanne Valette
Cover Design: Cornelia Niere, Munich
Production: Andrea Cobré
Separations: IGS
Printing and binding: Printer Portuguesa, Portugal

Printed in Portugal

ISBN 978-3-7913-8802-1

www.prestel.com